TRAIN YOUR BRAIN!

 **1**  **2**  **3**  **4** **5**

MATH GAMES

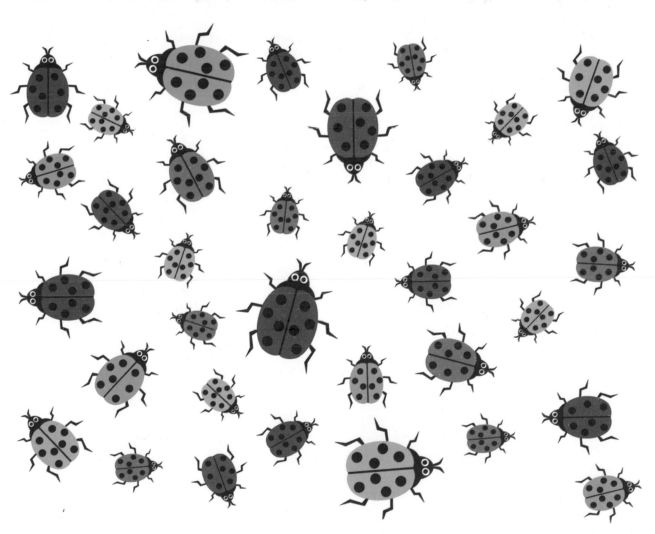

Illustrations: Michael Chung

Text: Alex Howe & Elizabeth Golding

Design: Anton Poitier

This book was conceived, created, and produced by iSeek Ltd. an imprint of Insight Editions

Insight Editions PO Box 3088 San Rafael, CA 94912

www.insighteditions.com

Library of Congress Cataloging-in-Publication Data available.

ISBN: 978-1-64722-422-6

Manufactured in China

10 9 8 7 6 5 4 3 2 1

Let's Get Started!

This book is jam-packed with amazing math puzzles. Some are easy, and some are much trickier. Each puzzle has a score, shown by the number on a robot:

See if you can solve each puzzle, and give yourself a score to add up when you finish. There is a maximum score of 235. Each time you score points, mark them off on this chart. Mark one gray line with a pencil for each point.

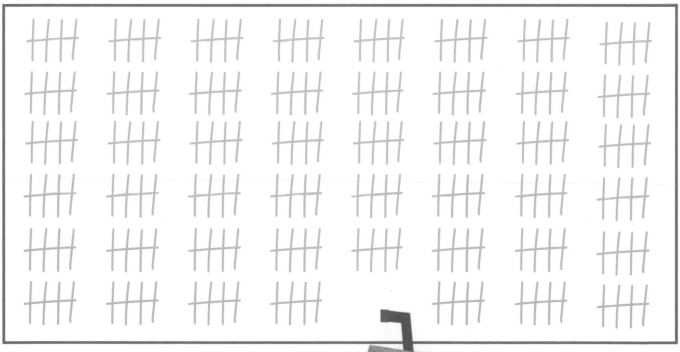

Take your time, and do the puzzles in any order you prefer. If you get stuck or want to check your work, the answers are at the back of the book.

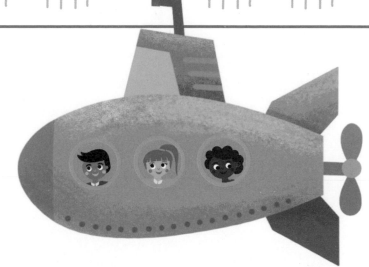

Cake Thief

Mr. Elephant made 10 cakes for Mrs. Elephant for when she came home. He made 5 chocolate cakes and 5 strawberry cakes.

When Mr. Elephant wasn't looking, Mr. Crocodile snuck in and ate 3 chocolate cakes and half of the strawberry cakes.

How many cakes were left for Mrs. Elephant?

Helicopter Rescue!

Four children are lost in a canyon and need to be rescued by helicopter! The helicopter can only fly up, down, left, or right. It can seat four people, plus the pilot.

The helicopter needs one gallon of fuel to fly the length of one square up, down, left, or right.

How much fuel does the helicopter need to rescue all four people and return safely?

Feeding Time at the Zoo

Tamsin the zookeeper needs to feed the monkeys their breakfast.

Each adult monkey needs two mangoes and three bananas, but the mommy monkey needs twice as much as the others. The baby needs only one banana. How much of each fruit does Tamsin need?

Bug Collection

Emily and Edward have a competition to see how many bugs they can collect. They each have score sheets to keep track of their points.

Use the score sheets to figure out who gets the most points for their bug collection.

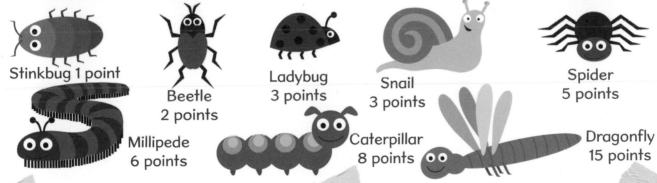

Stinkbug 1 point

Beetle 2 points

Ladybug 3 points

Snail 3 points

Spider 5 points

Millipede 6 points

Caterpillar 8 points

Dragonfly 15 points

Emily

Edward

Goal Grid

Emma is trying to score a goal.
She can only run up, down, left, or right.

How many squares does Emma need to run
through to score the goal, avoiding the defenders?
Start in the square that has the soccer ball.

Bee Squares

The bee needs to get to each colorful flower and then back to the hive to make honey! The bee can only fly up, down, left, or right.

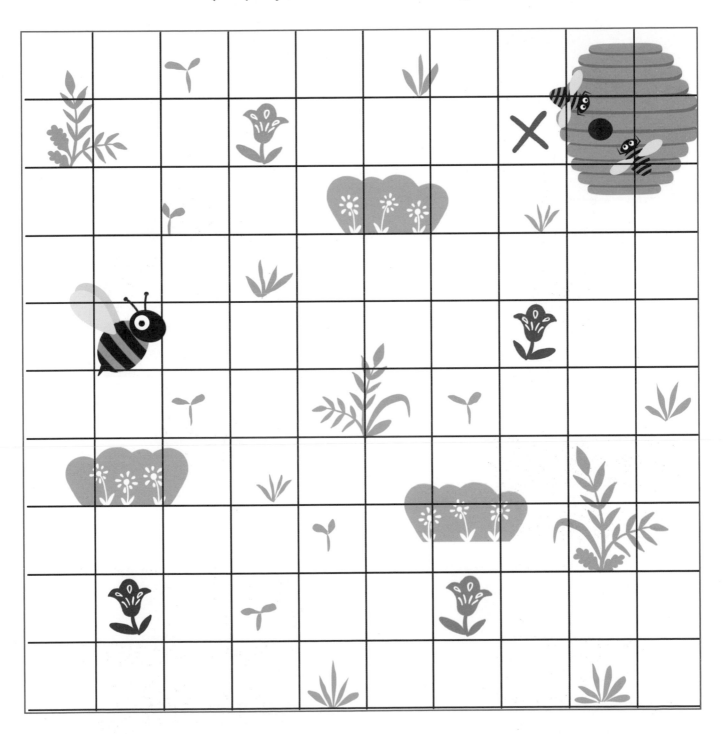

What is the fewest number of squares the bee needs to fly through to get to each flower and then back to the hive?

My Books

Ella has half as many books as her sister Sarah this year. Next year, Sarah will buy another four books and Ella will buy eight more books.

Sarah

Ella

How many books will they each have next year?

Picnic Basket

In the picnic basket, there are apples, sandwiches, bags of potato chips, and cartons of orange juice.

There are twice as many sandwiches as bags of potato chips.

There are three times as many apples as bags of potato chips.

There are half as many bags of potato chips as cartons of orange juice.

If there are four sandwiches, how many are there of each other item?

Bird Needs

Different birds need different amounts of seed in the bird feeder. Can you figure out which bird needs the most?

A robin needs a third of the amount of seeds a crow needs.

A pigeon needs twice as many seeds as a robin.

A crow needs 6 seeds.

If three of each bird visit the bird feeder, how many seeds need to be in it so that every bird gets fed?

Sandcastle Sums

Rahim's sandcastle has half as many pebbles as
Claire's castle, a third of the flags of Josh's castle, and
double the shells of Jessica's castle.

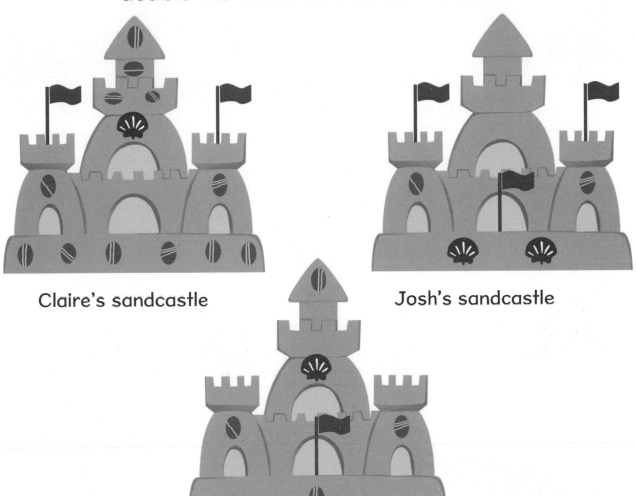

Claire's sandcastle   Josh's sandcastle

Jessica's sandcastle

Draw the right
number of each
decoration onto
Rahim's castle!

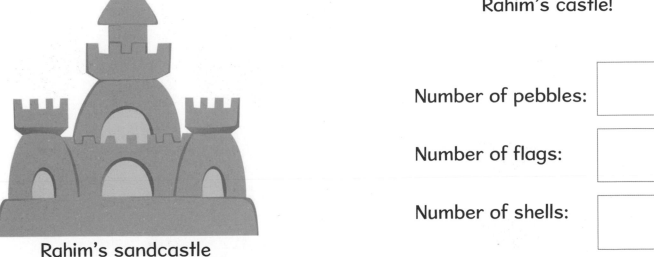

Rahim's sandcastle

Number of pebbles: ☐

Number of flags: ☐

Number of shells: ☐

Paper Planes

Harriet made paper planes using colored paper. She made four green planes, then she made some using orange, purple, red, and yellow paper. How many of each color did she make?

The number of green planes is the same as the number of purple planes.

There are twice as many orange planes as yellow.

TIP: We couldn't fit them all on the page, so counting won't help!

The number of yellow planes is a third of the number of red planes.

The number of purple planes is a third of the number of red planes.

Purple planes ☐

Yellow planes ☐

Orange planes ☐

Red planes ☐

All Aboard!

Each color train has a different number of cars. The green train is pulling into the station with two cars attached. There are three other trains. Add the right number of cars to each train.

The red train has triple the number of cars as the green train.

The blue train has half as many cars as the pink train.

The pink train has twice as many cars as the green train.

4

Fishy Fun

Eugene, Katie, and Will are in a
fish-spotting competition. Spotting each
fish is worth a certain amount of points.

Points

3 points   1 point   2 points   5 points

Eugene
I spot 4 yellow fish,
1 pink fish, and
1 blue fish.

Katie
I spot 4 pink fish,
2 blue fish, and
1 green fish.

Will
I spot 2 yellow fish,
3 green fish, and
1 blue fish.

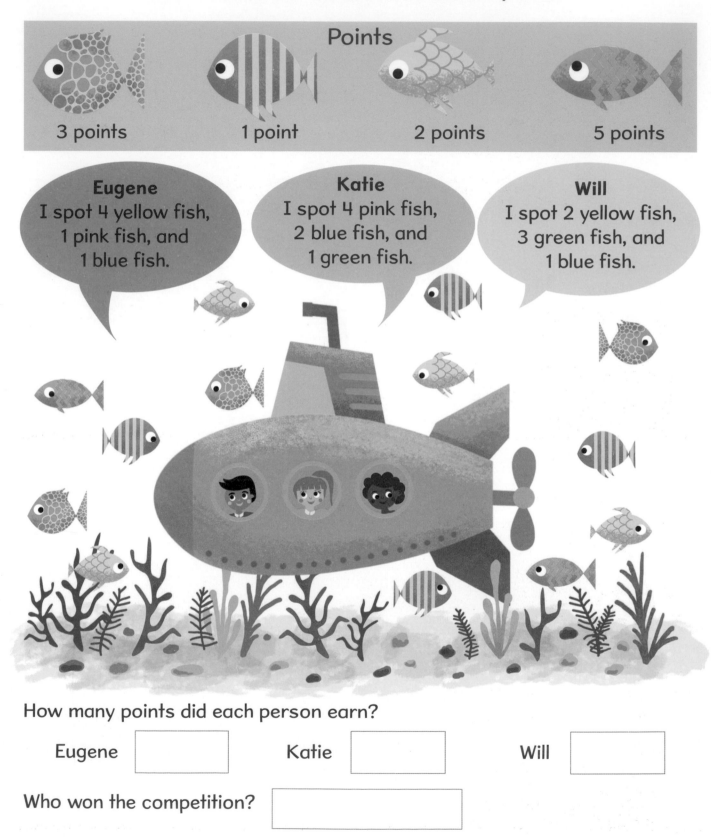

How many points did each person earn?

Eugene ☐   Katie ☐   Will ☐

Who won the competition? ☐

Space Score

Travis and Maya are having a competition using their telescopes. The chart shows how many points each one will earn for the things they see through their telescope.

Points

| 3 points | 1 point for each star | 2 points | 5 points |

Travis

Maya

How many points did each person earn?

Travis ____   Maya ____

Who won the competition? ____

Busy Baker

Becca has set up a bake sale and has a
price list for all her yummy treats.

Becca's Treats - PRICE LIST

$2.00	$1.00	$2.20
$1.20	$1.50	$2.50

Becca's first customer is her friend Bella. She buys a tray with all the
cakes below! How much does she pay? Her next customer is Joe. He
buys twice as many of the same cakes as Bella. What does he pay?

Bella paid: [   ]   Joe paid: [   ]

Dino Munch

Plant-eating dinosaurs had huge appetites! This chart shows how many trees they would eat in one day.

4 trees

3 trees

1 tree

2 trees

5 trees

2 trees

How many trees would the group of dinosaurs below eat in a day? How many would they eat in a week?

One day: [ ]   One week: [ ]

It's All Mine!

Three miners have found a lot of valuable gems in their mine. Which miner will make the most money?

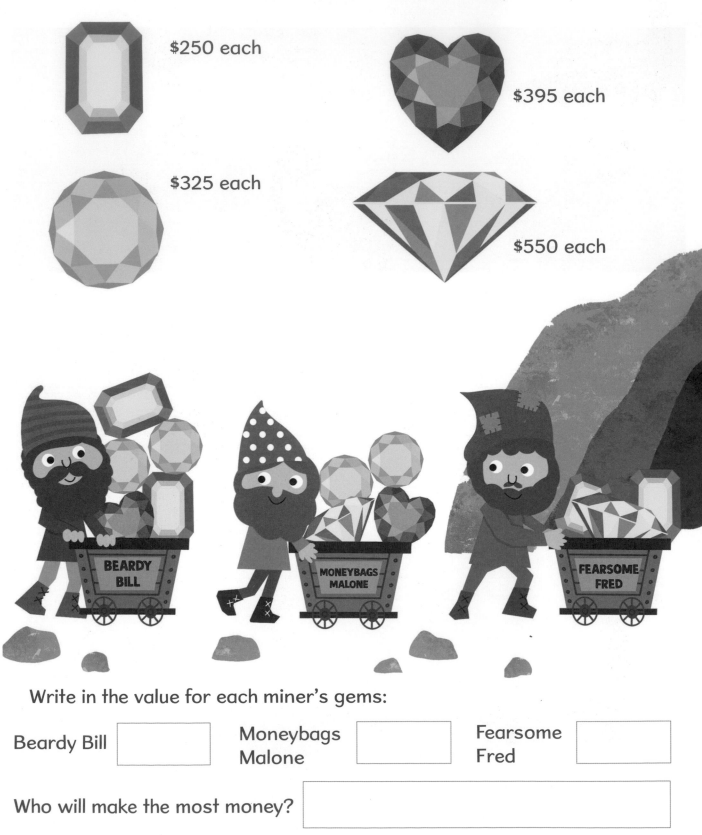

$250 each

$395 each

$325 each

$550 each

BEARDY BILL

MONEYBAGS MALONE

FEARSOME FRED

Write in the value for each miner's gems:

Beardy Bill [   ]

Moneybags Malone [   ]

Fearsome Fred [   ]

Who will make the most money? [   ]

Snake Sequence

These two snakes have numbers on their backs. Some of them are missing. Can you figure out the missing numbers?

Fill in the pink spaces.

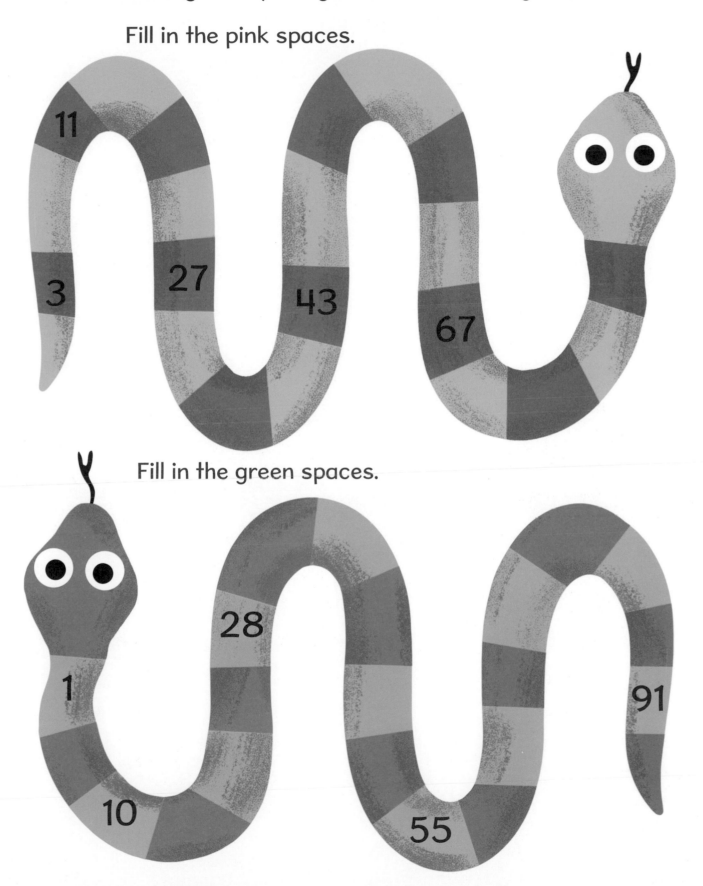

11

3

27

43

67

Fill in the green spaces.

1

28

91

10

55

Hopscotch Hop!

These hopscotch patterns start at the bottom and count upward. Fill in the gaps to complete the hopscotch sequence.

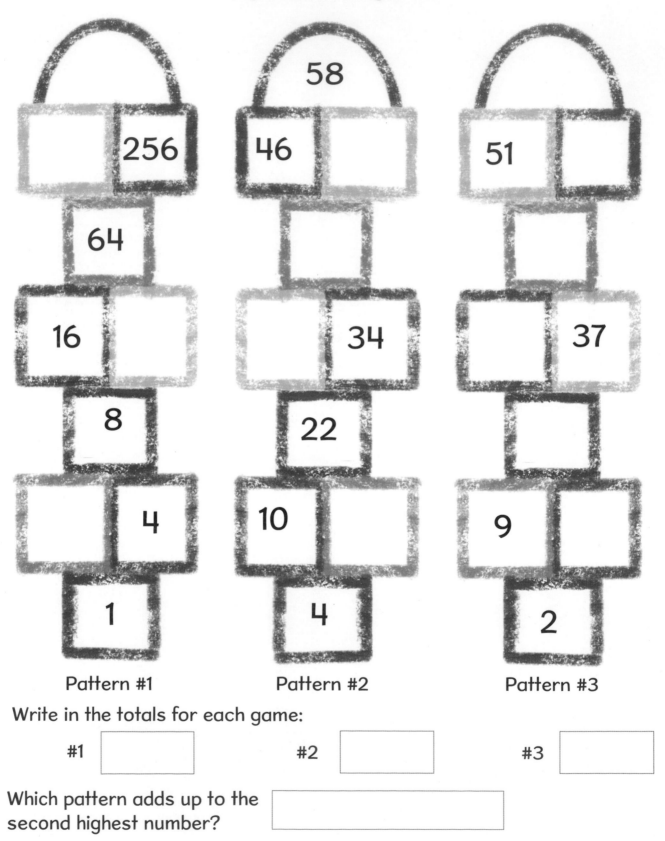

Pattern #1   Pattern #2   Pattern #3

Write in the totals for each game:

#1 [   ]   #2 [   ]   #3 [   ]

Which pattern adds up to the second highest number? [   ]

Eggstraordinary

Fill in the missing numbers on these rows of dinosaur eggs. Which row adds up to the highest number?

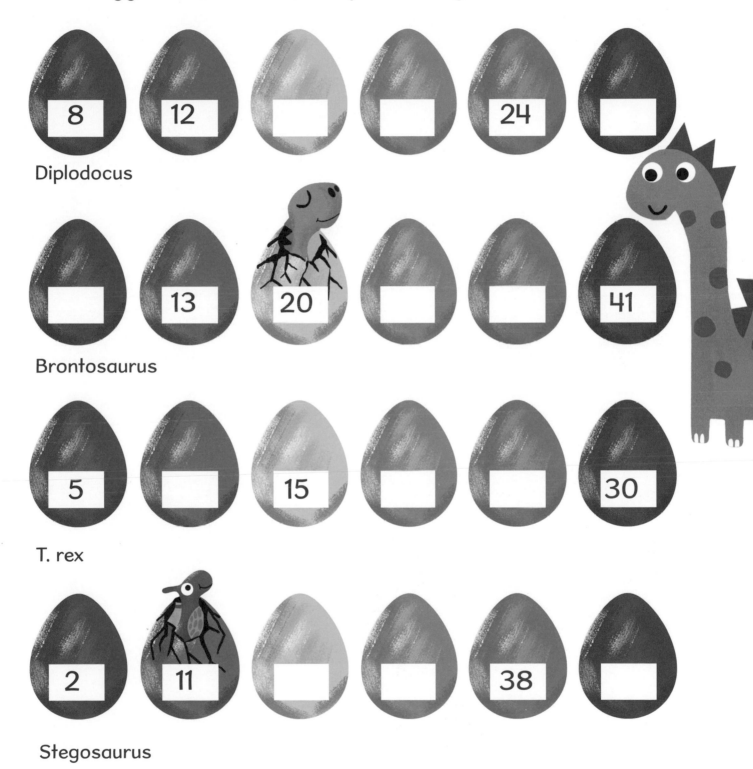

Diplodocus
8, 12, [ ], [ ], 24, [ ]

Brontosaurus
[ ], 13, 20, [ ], [ ], 41

T. rex
5, [ ], 15, [ ], 30

Stegosaurus
2, 11, [ ], [ ], 38, [ ]

The row with the highest number is: [ ]

Trip Total

Noah and Kate each have $25 to spend on their vacation.
One of them doesn't have enough to buy all the things
they want. Do they have enough money between them?
Will they have any change if they share their money?

Noah wants to buy
these things:

$6.00

$4.49

$6.25

$3.99

Kate wants to buy
these things:

$8.25

$12.75

$5.00

$2.25

Write in the total for each person: Noah [ ]   Kate [ ]

The total between
them is: [ ]

If they have any change,
how much do they have? [ ]

Ladybug Symmetry

There are lots of ladybugs on this page. Some are symmetrical (dots are the same on both sides), and some are not! Draw a circle around those that are not symmetrical.

How many asymmetrical ladybugs did you find?

Create-a-Crown

Finish drawing the crowns so that each side
is symmetrical (the same on both sides).
The first one has been done for you.

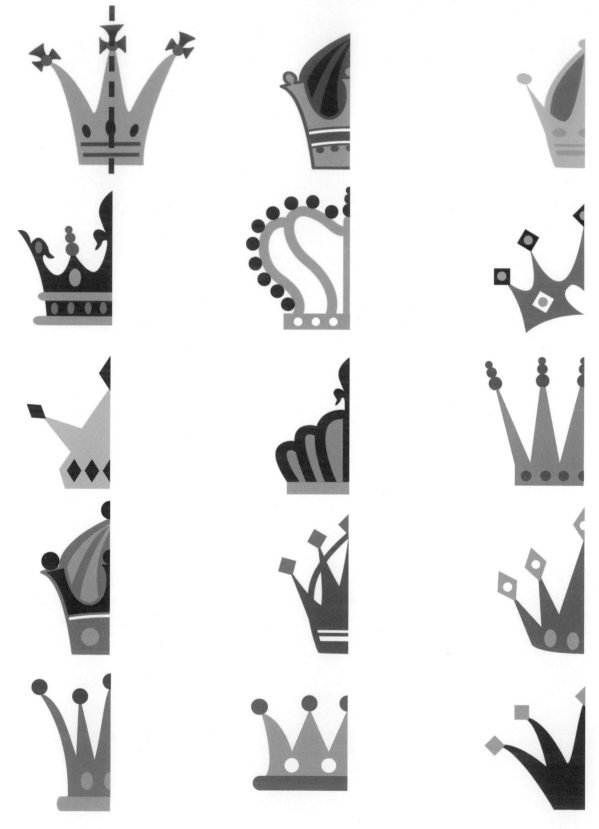

Dotted Lines

The line of symmetry is an imaginary line that divides a shape into equal sections. Draw the lines of symmetry onto the dice. The first two have been done for you!

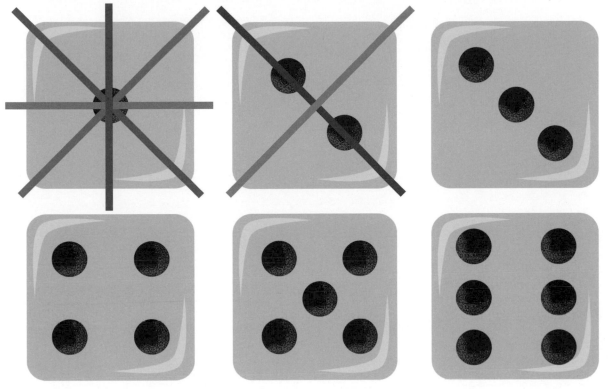

Now imagine that the blank dice below have 7, 8, 9, 10, 11, and 12 dots each. Draw the dots in place, then draw the lines of symmetry.

Pet Shop Prices

Four kids go to the pet shop and buy new pets.
Can you figure out the price of each pet?

I bought a turtle and a bird. I paid $55.00.

I bought three birds. I paid $54.00.

I bought two guinea pigs and a goldfish. I paid $45.50.

I bought two goldfish and a turtle. I paid $48.00.

Fill in the correct price for each animal in the pet shop.
One has been done for you.

$18.00

Shoe Shopping

Ben and Tara go to the shoe store to get new shoes for school. Who spends the most money?

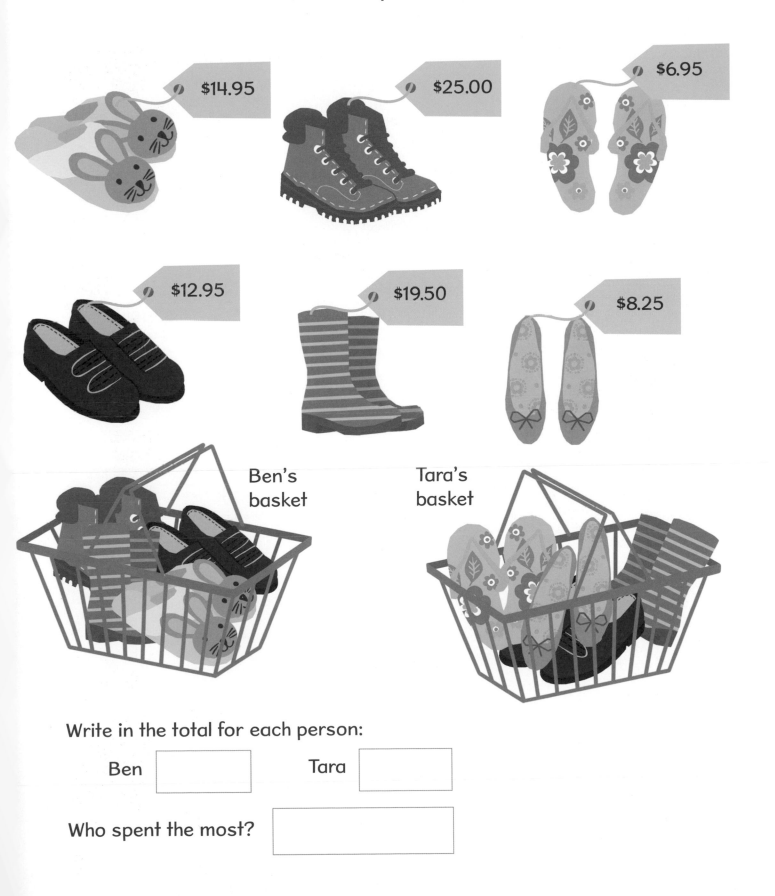

$14.95

$25.00

$6.95

$12.95

$19.50

$8.25

Ben's basket

Tara's basket

Write in the total for each person:

Ben

Tara

Who spent the most?

Flow Time

The gardener is trying to water the plants, but each of these hoses has kinks in it, reducing water flow. Figure out the number of gallons that get to the plants by dividing the flow each time.

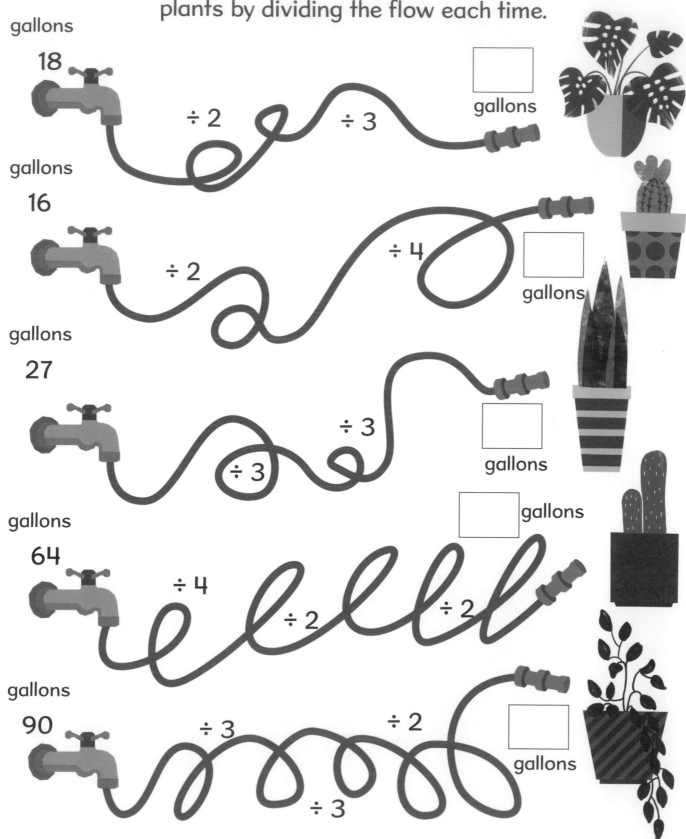

gallons
18
÷ 2   ÷ 3
gallons

gallons
16
÷ 2   ÷ 4
gallons

gallons
27
÷ 3   ÷ 3
gallons

gallons
64
÷ 4   ÷ 2   ÷ 2
gallons

gallons
90
÷ 3   ÷ 2   ÷ 3
gallons

Snail Sums

These snails are looking for their shells! Figure out which shell belongs to which snail, and write the correct shell number above each snail.

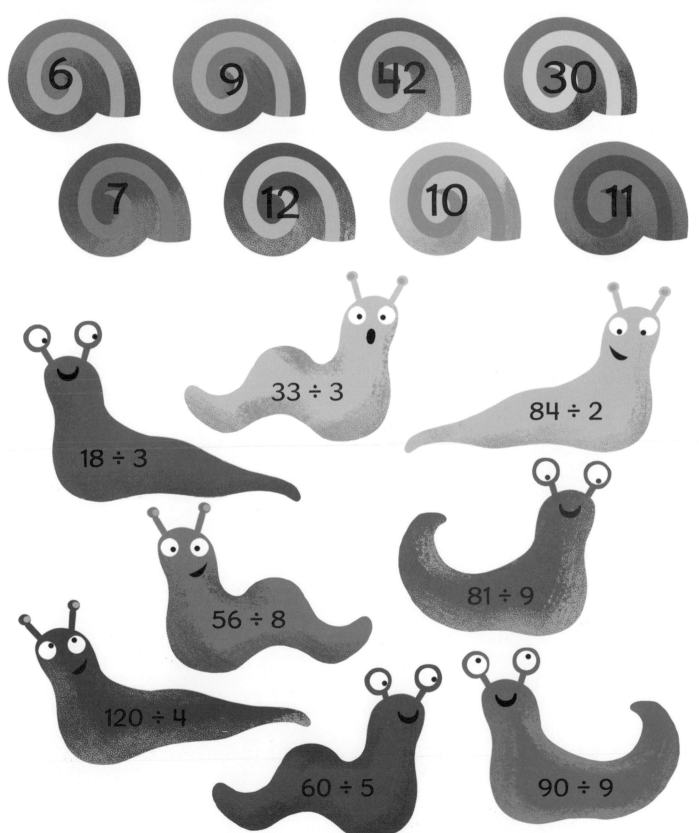

Space Shuffle

Each spacecraft takes off with some astronauts on board, then picks up more from a space station before landing on a planet. Draw a line from each spacecraft to the station and the planet where they land.

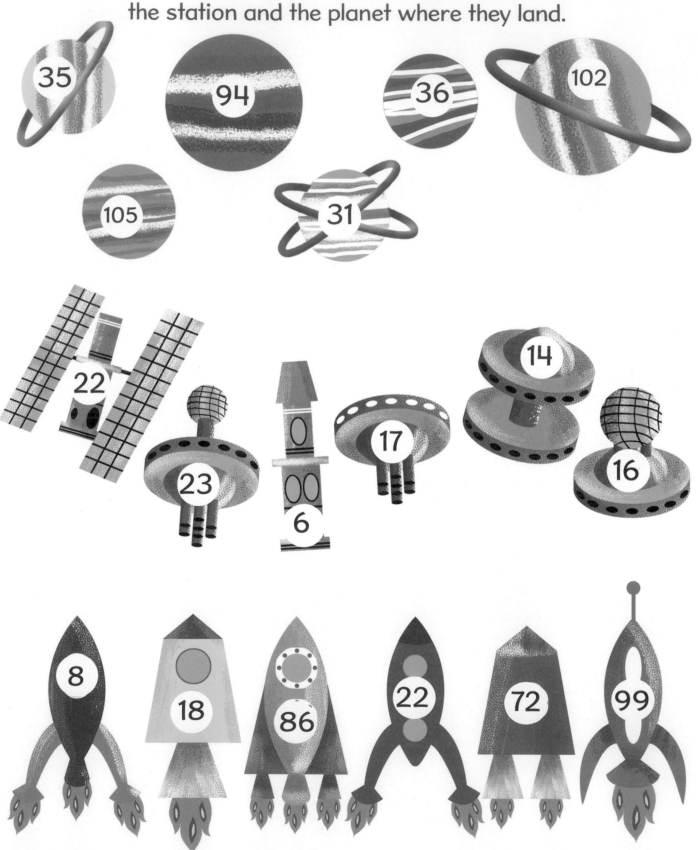

Counting Sheep

A sleepy farmer needs help to finish counting his sheep. He counts them in 3s on Monday, 4s on Tuesday, 5s on Wednesday, 6s on Thursday, 7s on Friday, 8s on Saturday, and 9s on Sunday. How many sheep did he have to count each night? Monday has been done for you.

This was the number he counted up to before he fell asleep.

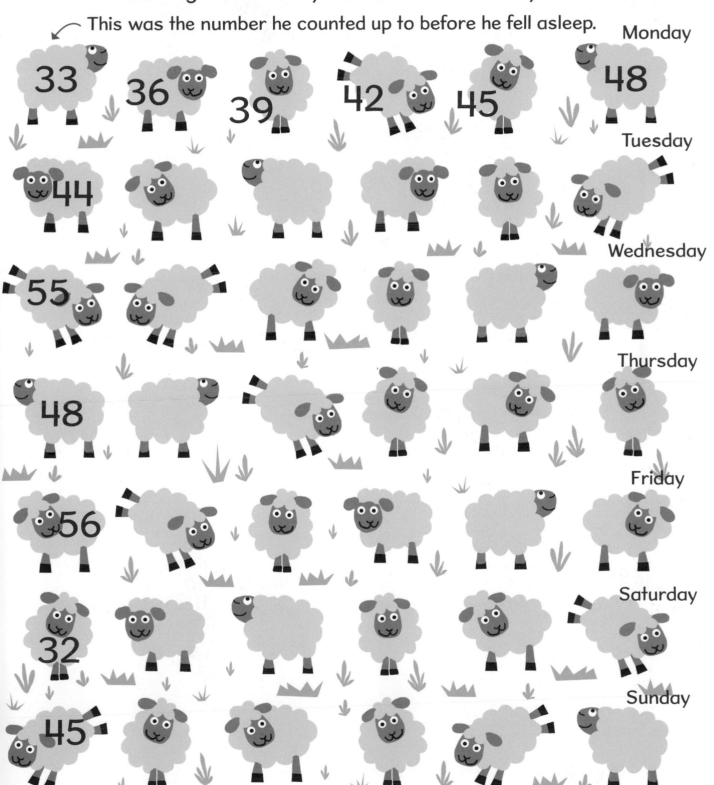

Monday

33 36 39 42 45 48

Tuesday

44

Wednesday

55

Thursday

48

Friday

56

Saturday

32

Sunday

45

Umbrella Sums

Each segment of each umbrella contains a multiple of the number at the tip. Fill in the blanks! The first one has been done for you.

4

Umbrella 1 (tip 5): 5, 10, 15, 20, 25

Umbrella 2 (tip 7): 7, _, 21, _, 35

Umbrella 3: _, 16, _, 32, _

Umbrella 4 (tip 3): _, _, 9, 12, _

Umbrella 5 (tip 2): 2, _, _, 8, _

Umbrella 6 (tip 4): 4, _, _, 16, _

Umbrella 7 (tip 12): 12, _, 24, _

Umbrella 8 (tip 11): 11, _, 33, _

Decorator Math

Choose the decorations for this tree by matching the sums to the right answer. Draw lines between them.

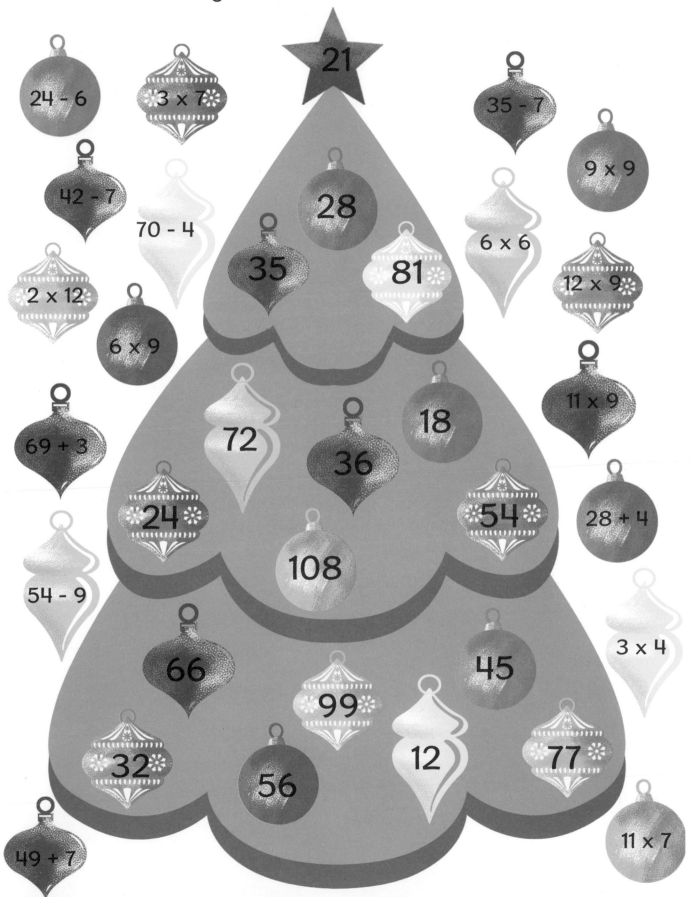

24 - 6

3 x 7

35 - 7

42 - 7

9 x 9

70 - 4

6 x 6

2 x 12

12 x 9

6 x 9

11 x 9

69 + 3

28 + 4

54 - 9

3 x 4

49 + 7

11 x 7

21

28

35

81

72

36

18

24

54

108

66

45

99

12

77

32

56

All Squared Up

Match the shapes to make eight squares.
Draw lines between the matches.
Hint: The colors might not match!

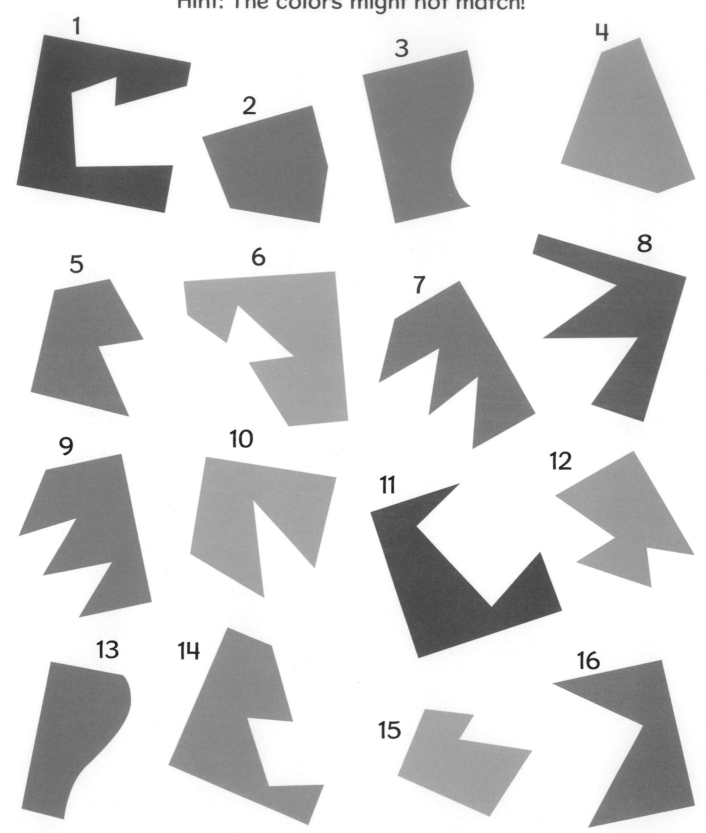

All Cracked Up

Match these broken eggshells to make eight
complete eggs. Draw lines between the matches.
Hint: The colors might not match!

Rectangle Roundup

Match these broken rectangle shapes to make nine complete rectangles. Each is broken into three pieces. Hint: To help you, two of the colors in each rectangle match.

Circle Search

Match these broken circle shapes to make five complete circles. Each is broken into four pieces. Hint: To help you, two of the colors in each circle match.

Citrus Fractions

Lemons and oranges have been cut in half to show the segments. Each fruit has eight equal parts.

$\dfrac{2}{4}$ Circle all the fruits with a blue pencil that show this fraction: two-fourths

$\dfrac{1}{2}$ Circle all the fruits with a blue pencil that show this fraction: one half

$\dfrac{5}{8}$ Circle all the fruits with a green pencil that show this fraction: five-eighths

$\dfrac{7}{8}$ Circle all the fruits with an orange pencil that show this fraction: seven-eighths

$\dfrac{1}{4}$ Circle all the fruits with a purple pencil that show this fraction: one quarter

$\dfrac{2}{8}$ Circle all the fruits with a purple pencil that show this fraction: two-eighths

Which of the fractions above are the same amounts?

Spy Sums

Superspy Agent Zero is stealing secret documents! Follow her to see how many documents she delivers to base.

5:00 am: Agent Zero breaks into government HQ and steals 78 documents.

6:00 am: She's spotted by a security dog and is chased, dropping 7 documents.

6:45 am: At the next office, she steals 27 documents but accidentally shreds 3 when she confuses the shredder with a copier!

7:15 am: Agent Zero breaks open a safe and steals another 102 documents.

7:45 am: She leaves the office and drops 3 documents. One gets stuck to her foot.

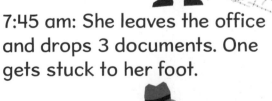

8:00 am: Safely back at mission base, she puts all the documents on Inspector Zed's desk.

Zed's desk

How many documents does Agent Zero put on Inspector Zed's desk?

Shape Spotter

How many triangles, squares, and pentagons can you find?

Write the number you found in the corresponding shapes:

Shape Sorter

These five shapes are in a jumble. Can you figure out how many there are of each? Write the number in each of the corresponding shapes at the bottom.

X Marks the Spot!

The pirates have buried treasure in eight places on these islands. Locate and mark all the treasure, then add up the value. Hint: Read the X-AXIS first.

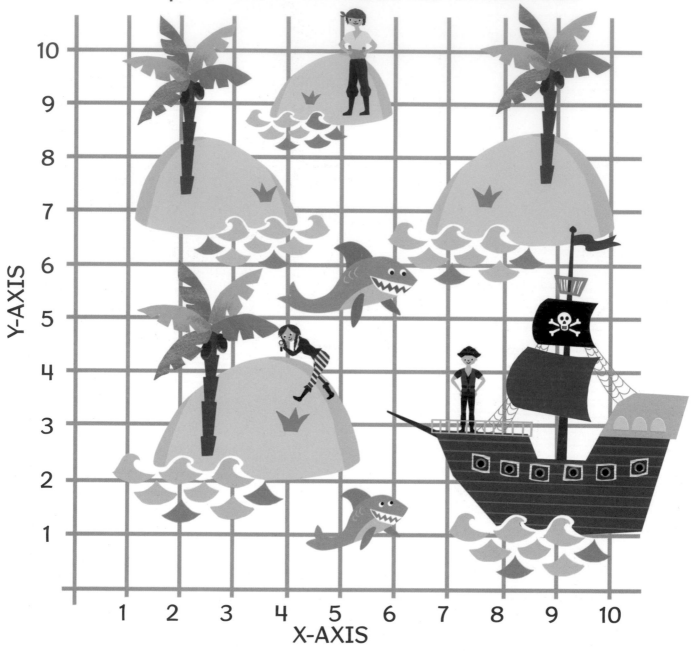

$250 of gold is buried at 3, 4.

$920 of diamonds are buried at 9, 7

$432 of silver is buried at 5, 3

$225 of gold is buried at 3, 8

$700 of treasure is buried at 2, 7

$150 of silver is buried at 2, 3

$171 of sapphires are buried at 4, 9

$122 of gold is buried at 8, 8

What is all the treasure worth?

Buried Bones

Three dogs have buried bones in the yard. Each bone weighs one pound. Can you figure out where the bones are buried and how many? Hint: Read the X-AXIS first.

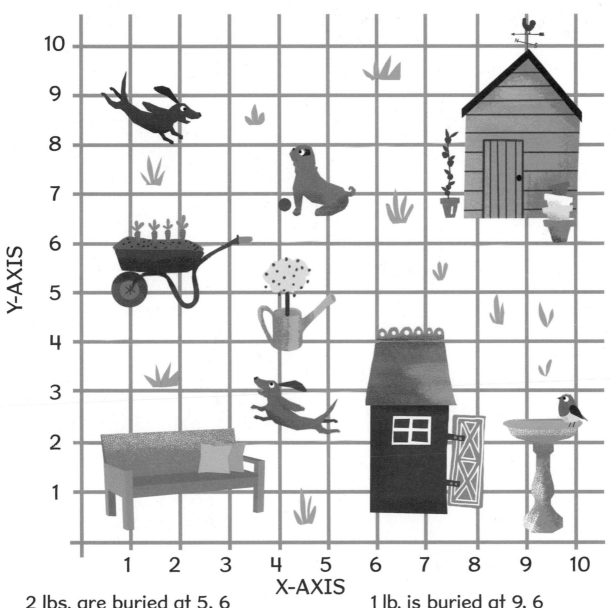

2 lbs. are buried at 5, 6

1 lb. is buried at 7, 9

3 lbs. are buried at 6, 5

4 lbs. are buried at 8, 3

1 lb. is buried at 9, 6

2 lbs. are buried at 5, 9

1 lb. is buried at 3, 7

3 lbs. are buried at 4, 10

How many bones did they bury?

Watermelon Mix-Up

Most of these slices of watermelon have the same number of seeds, but some of them have a different number. Draw a circle around the odd ones.

If every slice of watermelon had five seeds, how many seeds would there be in total?

Tall Order

Several giraffe families have gotten separated. Each family group will have the same number of spots. How many families can you find?

How many giraffe families did you find?

Crab Counting

There are 100 crabs in 8 different colors. Count and sort them into groups by color. Which color group has the most crabs and which has the least?

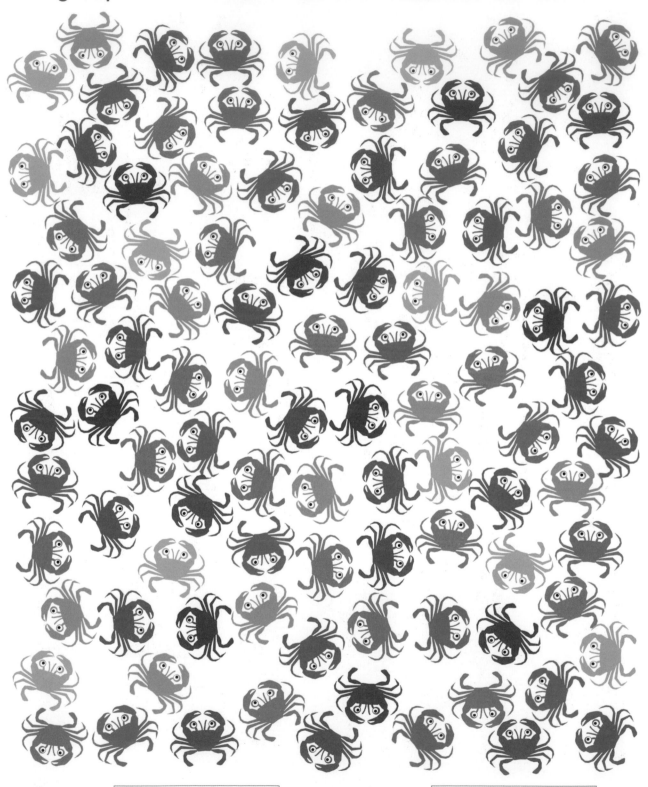

Most crabs: _____   Least crabs: _____

Bee Careful!

There are 200 bees on this page. If 100 bees fly away, and then a quarter of the remaining bees go to sleep, how many will be left to visit the flowers?

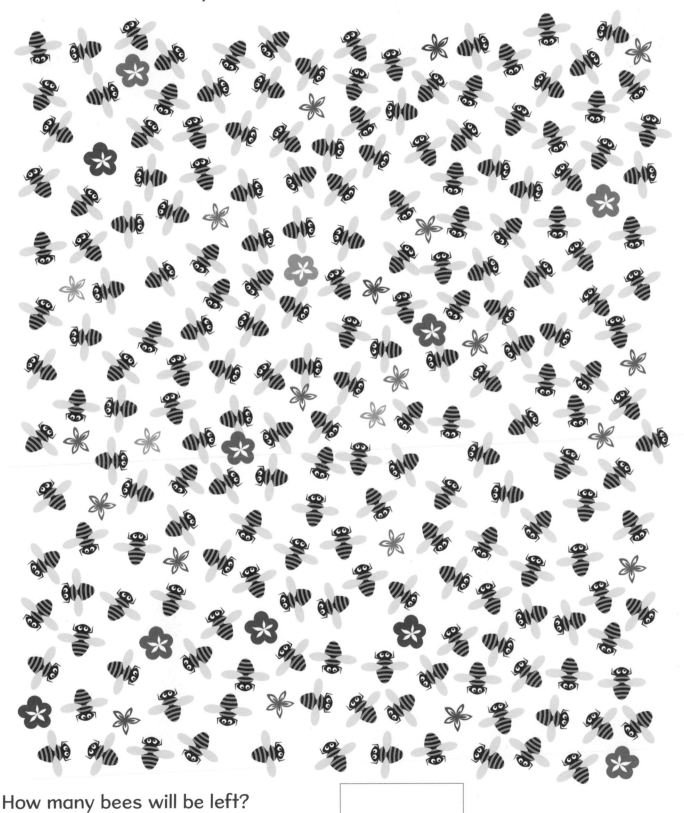

How many bees will be left?

2-D Drawing Challenge

Draw a haunted house in 2-D using these shapes.
Add some ghosts and goblins just for fun!

circle   square   triangle   rectangle   semi-circle   oval

3-D Drawing Challenge

Draw a castle in 3-D using these shapes. Give your castle a name, and add a king and queen just for fun!

sphere

cube

cone

cuboid

pyramid

cylinder

Cupcake Challenge

Two kids baked some cupcakes together. They each have four friends. They decided to give each of their friends six cupcakes. Then they each ate two themselves.

Did they have enough cupcakes for everyone?

If any cupcakes were left over, how many were there?

Taking Turns

These planes are lining up for takeoff. Each jet must wait four minutes before taking off. The propeller planes must wait three minutes. The first plane takes off at 12:30 pm.

first plane in line

last plane in line

What time does the first propeller plane take off?

What time does the last plane take off?

Roman Numerals

This chart shows the Roman numerals from 1 to 20.
Use the chart to figure out the answers.

1	2	3	4	5	6	7	8	9	10
I	II	III	IV	V	VI	VII	VIII	IX	X
11	12	13	14	15	16	17	18	19	20
XI	XII	XIII	XIV	XV	XVI	XVII	XVIII	XIX	XX

Write the numbers next the Roman numerals.

II =   IX =

V =   XII =

X =   VI =

XI =   XVII =

VII =   IV =

XIII =   XVI =

Write the Roman numerals next to the numbers.

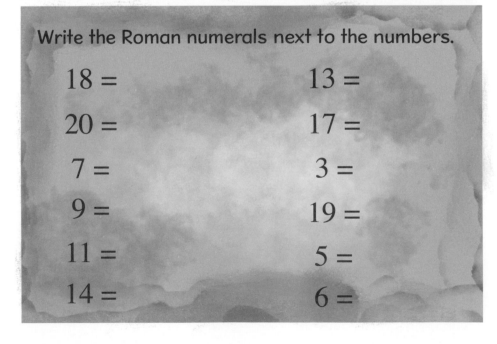

18 =   13 =

20 =   17 =

7 =   3 =

9 =   19 =

11 =   5 =

14 =   6 =

Clock Work

Refer to the Roman numerals chart to draw the hands in the correct positions on each of these clocks.

2:45 pm

5:15 pm

3:20 pm

10:30 am

11:50 am

9:30 am

7:15 pm

12:30 pm

4:45 pm

Counting Carrots

The little gray rabbit wants to eat the
carrots that are growing in the garden.

How many carrots will be left if the rabbit eats these fractions of them?

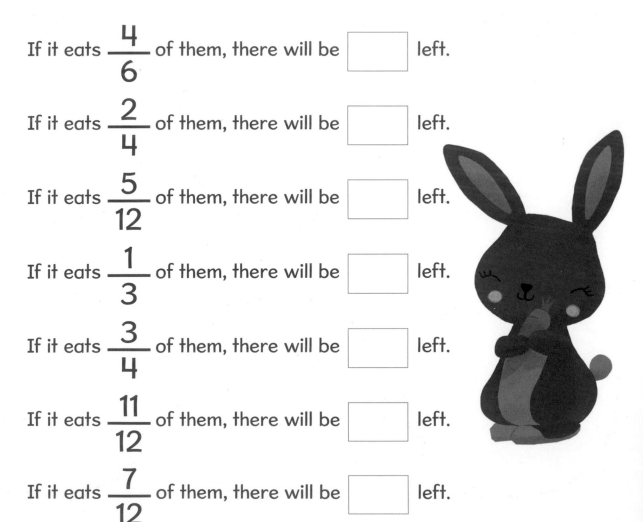

If it eats $\dfrac{4}{6}$ of them, there will be ☐ left.

If it eats $\dfrac{2}{4}$ of them, there will be ☐ left.

If it eats $\dfrac{5}{12}$ of them, there will be ☐ left.

If it eats $\dfrac{1}{3}$ of them, there will be ☐ left.

If it eats $\dfrac{3}{4}$ of them, there will be ☐ left.

If it eats $\dfrac{11}{12}$ of them, there will be ☐ left.

If it eats $\dfrac{7}{12}$ of them, there will be ☐ left.

Domino Fractions

Look at the shape pictures on each domino and write each one as a fraction next to the picture. Some fractions have been done for you.

Where's the Beach?

This surfer needs help finding the beach. Figure out the number sequence to mark the route the surfer should take to the beach. The first three have been done for you.

Follow the Footsteps

This dinosaur needs help following the footsteps to the forest. Figure out the number sequence to mark the path the dino should take. The first three have been done for you.

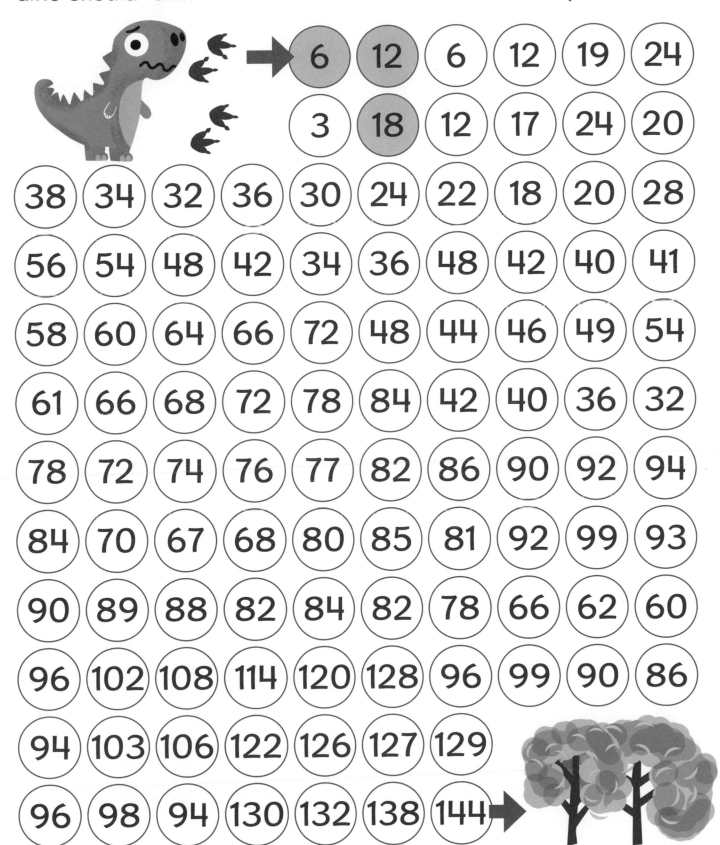

	➡	**6**	**12**	6	12	19	24		
		3	**18**	12	17	24	20		
38	34	32	36	30	24	22	18	20	28
56	54	48	42	34	36	48	42	40	41
58	60	64	66	72	48	44	46	49	54
61	66	68	72	78	84	42	40	36	32
78	72	74	76	77	82	86	90	92	94
84	70	67	68	80	85	81	92	99	93
90	89	88	82	84	82	78	66	62	60
96	102	108	114	120	128	96	99	90	86
94	103	106	122	126	127	129			
96	98	94	130	132	138	144 ➡			

$4\frac{1}{2}$

28 gallons

16 mangoes
25 bananas

35 points | 26 points

11 squares

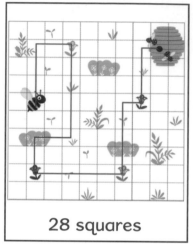

28 squares

Sarah: 18, Ella: 15

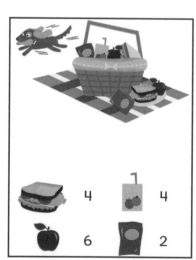

4
4
6
2

The crow, 36 seeds

6 pebbles,
1 flag,
2 shells

4
8
4
12

14, 17, 18, Will

15, 17, Maya

$15.40, $30.80

20, 140

$1,545, $1,595, $1,050
Moneybags Malone

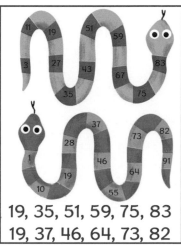

19, 35, 51, 59, 75, 83
19, 37, 46, 64, 73, 82

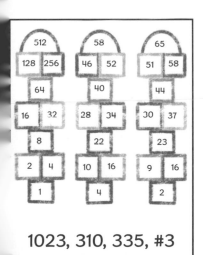

1023, 310, 335, #3

Stegosaurus

$20.73, $28.25
$48.98, $1.02

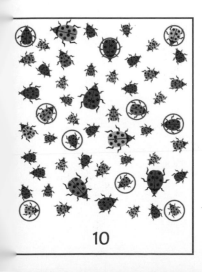

10

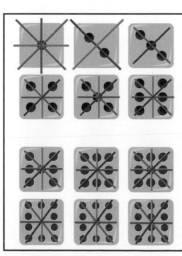

$72.40, $47.65, Ben

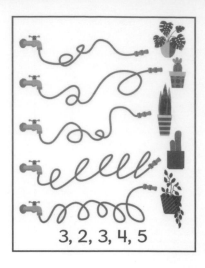

3, 2, 3, 4, 5

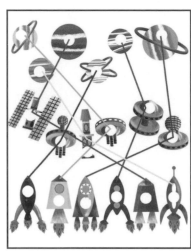

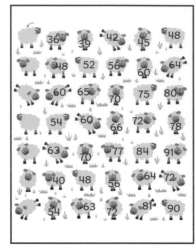

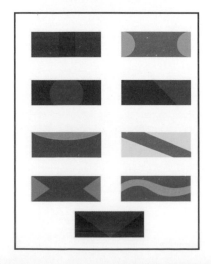

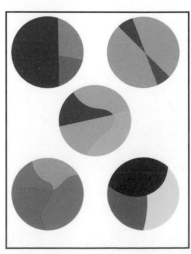

$$\frac{1}{4} \, \& \, \frac{2}{8} \qquad \frac{2}{4} \, \& \, \frac{1}{2}$$

195 including the one on her foot.

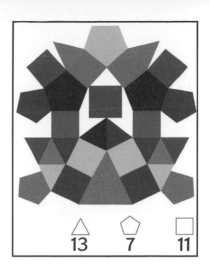

△ 13   ⬠ 7   ☐ 11

■ 5   ▲ 4   ▮ 4   ● 5   ⬠ 4

$2,970

17 bones

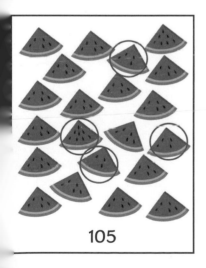

105

5

dark green, red

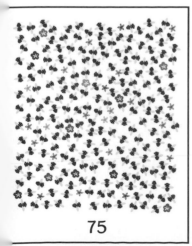

75

There are many possible outcomes

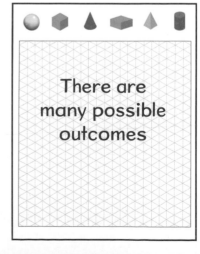

There are many possible outcomes

Yes, 8

12:41, 1:20

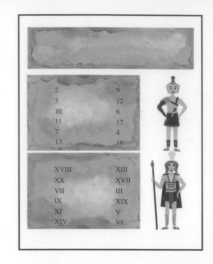

4, 6, 7, 8, 3, 1, 5

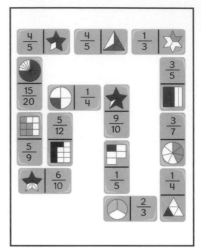

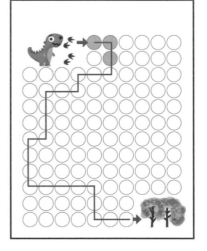

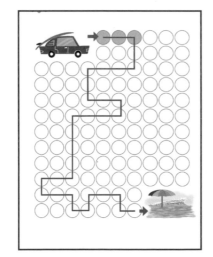